Seamus Sherlock

The Fight of My Life

By

Marisa Reidy

Dedication

I dedicate this book to the thousands of families who have faced eviction in Ireland through the generations.

Acknowledgements

First and foremost, to my wonderful children and extended family: Thank you for your unwavering love and support and for standing with me through what was the toughest time of my life.

To my friends and neighbours and every single person who came to the gate to stand with me. Those who sent emails, text messages, and made phone calls in support of what I was doing. Every single one of you played a massive part in this story, and your support will always mean the world to me.

To my family members who were deceased before I took my stand against eviction. I always felt that you were with me through it all, and I have no doubt that you all kept me going through the darkest days.

To my partner, Andrea: Working alongside you is an amazing experience. Your knowledge of breeding and producing sports horses is a testament to the wonderful person you are. Thank You.

And finally, to Marisa – the lady who agreed to write my story. I am really delighted that Marisa agreed to write this book. Our first meeting with Marisa was a few days after we closed the gate when she came to cover the story for The Kerryman Newspaper. She was so kind and thoughtful in the way she covered our story and immediately put us at ease. When we decided to write this book, I always felt that I wanted the right words to go down in history, and Marisa did that. The fact that Marisa agreed to write this book is the reason we did it. Without her, there would not have been a book.

About the Author

Marisa Reidy is a native of County Kerry, currently living in Abbeydorney with her husband Declan and 12-year-old daughter, Hanna.

Now working part-time as PR & Marketing Officer for cancer support charity, Recovery Haven Kerry, Marisa's background is in Journalism. With a degree in Irish and Media & Communication Studies from the University of Limerick, Marisa worked as a news journalist for *The Kerryman Newspaper* from 1999 to 2016 before taking time out to care full-time for her daughter, who has Cystic Fibrosis.

During her time with *The Kerryman*, Marisa won three journalism awards, including the National Newspapers of Ireland (NNI) Regional Journalist of the Year accolade in 2012 and two Justice Media Awards for court reporting in 2012 and 2016.

In her current role with Recovery Haven, Marisa won the 2019 *Connect Kerry* Women In Business Award in Marketing, Events & PR.

It was while working with *The Kerryman Newspaper* that Marisa first met Seamus Sherlock and covered his story extensively and was thrilled when Seamus approached her in 2020 to write his book.

Table of Contents

Dedication ii

Acknowledgements iii

About the Author v

The Eviction Letter and the Immediate Aftermath 1

How It All Came Undone… 14

The debt & Despair Was Everywhere 21

My Year of Hell on Earth 32

The Fear And Anxiety Almost Led Me To Suicide 40

Dividing Opinion 47

It's All Over… 59

End of An Era 69

Was It All Really Worth It? 73

The Eviction Letter and the Immediate Aftermath

"I genuinely believed my kids would be better off without a failure like me."

Seamus with his sons JJ & Dermot manning the barricade at Appletown Farm in 2012. Photo by John Reidy

Thursday, August 16th, 2012, began as a pretty normal day for 46-year-old Seamus Sherlock. He was up early; his animals on Appleltown Farm in West Limerick were fed, and the two youngest of his five children had left for school.

Money worries were always something that played on Seamus' mind, as he had fallen behind on his mortgage a few years previously, but they didn't weigh any heavier that day than any other.

That afternoon, as he returned home from Newcastle West, where he had just bought his weekly stock of animal feed and dog nuts for his rescue dogs, Seamus – as he did most days – stopped to check the post box at the gate. Just a few customary brown envelopes again, which he assumed meant more bills. Little did he know then, however, that one envelope, in particular, was to change his life immeasurably.

"I said I'd open it while I was at the letterbox, and the first word I saw was *execution*," Seamus recalls. "I said to myself, *'what the hell is this…is this some kind of a joke?'* And when I read it again and again, the word 'execution' was on the letter three times."

That fateful letter was from the county registrar – or the Sheriff's office, as Seamus called it. The letter stated that an 'order of execution' had been lodged in the office against him and that said order would be enforced without any further notice to him.

"I actually read it three or four times. I couldn't get my head around it. It was a complete bolt out of the blue. I really wasn't expecting anything like this," he recalls. "It was then I started to realise that this is some kind of an eviction notice.

"So I rang the number on the letter and spoke to a nice, pleasant chap and asked him straight out if this was an eviction notice."

The man on the phone confirmed Seamus' worst fears.

Panicked, shaken, and unsure exactly what this meant, Seamus asked when the eviction was going to happen, and the reply he received is something he says he will never forget.

"He just said *'today, tomorrow, whenever'* and told me that if I was willing to go voluntarily, they'd let us take our clothes. I'll never forget the feeling. I started imagining all sorts of things - people coming and dragging my children and me out of that house or even shooting my animals – because I'd heard some awful stories."

That phone call, and the fear of what might happen, would trigger a major turning point for Seamus. He says he decided there and then that he was never going to stand back and let anyone put himself, but importantly his children, in danger.

"The minute I hung up the phone, my attitude completely changed," Seamus admits. "I hung up the phone and decided that I had to protect my family."

Sick to his stomach with fear and noticing his heart beating frighteningly fast, a terrified Seamus realised the magnitude of what had just happened.

"I rarely get panic attacks, but I know I got one after hanging up from that call because my heart was thumping out of the chest. I said, *'Oh my God, this is going to be awful. My children are going to be homeless. I'm going to be homeless.'* The fact that I wasn't expecting it was the biggest shock," Seamus recalls.

"For 15 minutes, I felt like I couldn't breathe. I didn't know what I was going to do. I physically couldn't get back into the jeep to drive it up the passageway. My head was spinning. I didn't know if they'd be here in an hour or what."

Having steadied himself, Seamus drove his jeep up to the house. There, his five children - Mary Kate (13), Bridget (18), Bernadette (19) and sons JJ (14) and Dermot (21) - were going about their business, completely oblivious to what had just happened. Seamus was separated at the time, and the children lived with him full-time but split their time between the farm and their mother's home.

Then came an unimaginable conversation – a conversation no father ever wants to have with his children.

"I remember telling them that we were in a bit of bother - that it looks like we're going to be evicted," Seamus recalls, visibly upset. "There was a silence in the room. They didn't know what I was talking about. I told them straight away that I wanted to save this farm and that I was determined to pay for it, but that they would have to go and stay with their mother because these people could hurt them. Imagine having to tell your children that.

"I remember Bridget saying to me, *'What do you mean they'll hurt us?'* and I said that they could come in the middle of the night and drag them by the hair of the head down the stairs. She turned to me and said: *'By God, dad, they won't.'*

An agonising conversation followed between Seamus and his children, all of whom were determined to stand with their father - whatever that meant.

"We talked about it for a long time and discussed how I'd try to put a plan in place to pay for the farm. They knew I was in arrears and that I was trying to pay for it, but when I lost my bog in 2008, I couldn't meet the full repayments. We were surviving but living hand to mouth, really. It was tight, but it wasn't poverty.

"I remember clearly telling them that I would have to stand up to this, and they said they'd stand with me. They said we either do it as a team or we don't do it at all. I rarely ever cry, but I did at that moment. There were a thousand emotions going through my head at one time. I was terrified that they were going to be hurt but so proud that they were standing up. My emotions were going a thousand times a minute."

A mixture of pride, defiance, anger and determination immediately took hold, and Seamus and his older sons began constructing a barricade of silage bales at the entrance to the farm – a stark image that would very soon be broadcast across media channels and newspapers the length and breadth of the country and further afield.

"We got 30 bales of silage and put them up against the gate. But then we didn't know what the hell to do," Seamus recalls. "I rang a few friends and told them what was happening. Slowly, they rang other friends, and the media got hold of it. I remember a chap from a radio station in Limerick arrived with a microphone in his hand, and he asked me for a few words. I spoke to him, and I'll always remember him turning to JJ and asking him why he was there with me. He simply said: *'I'm standing with my father.'* I couldn't control my emotions. These were young kids. I remember at that exact moment feeling so upset and embarrassed that I was putting my kids through this."

Seamus describes the first night behind the barricade as the longest and most terrifying night of his life. It was also one of the darkest mental experiences he had ever endured.

"I had a legally held shotgun, and I stood at the gate with my dog Rosie, with the shotgun on the bales. I couldn't sleep. I wasn't ever going to use the gun, but it was there. It was the longest night of my life. The reason *I* was standing there was that they were coming for *me,* and I wanted to keep them away from the children. But looking back, if they were coming for me, they would probably have gone in and got the kids anyway. It was absolute terror. I didn't know if they'd bring the armed police – and I was standing here with a sheepdog! I kept thinking, '*I must be some failure to be putting my kids through this. Sure, only a failure would go on this way.*' I genuinely believed my kids would be better off without a failure like me.

"I remember thinking that I had no idea how I would handle it if I saw them swinging in the gate. I was on my own, so I had no hope. But I did say to myself: '*I'd sooner die than walk out of here in the wrong,*' so I suppose I kept telling myself that."

Seamus admits that he had convinced himself that he might die protecting his property – such was his determination not to lose the farm that he was genuinely trying to pay for. A farm that he had invested blood, sweat and tears into saving.

"I did, in my foolishness, think they were going to kill me because, as far as I was concerned, it was the only way they were going to get me out. Every minute was like an hour. I could see the lights of every car on the road, and every time I saw those lights, I thought it could be them. My heart was racing every time I saw a light. That first night was the hardest of my life, without a doubt. But I was thinking that if they got me, they might let the kids alone."

As the hours passed, Seamus' mind again wandered to the harrowing conversation he had had with the older boys about what his stand could mean for them. His sons, in particular, were standing by their father at any cost, and this is something that caused him untold anxiety and fear.

"My only concern was that I knew my boys wouldn't leave my side, so I was petrified that if I was being beaten or attacked, they would have jumped in. I warned them that if it gets to the stage that I'm on the ground and guys in balaclavas are beating me, not to try and save me," an emotional Seamus recalls.

"They just said, '*Are you joking, da*?' And I know if it was my dad, nothing would have stopped me. They were petrified out of their minds, of course. It's your worst nightmare. The thought of it alone must have been horrendous for them, but the only reason I said it was because I was afraid it would happen because I had heard of it happening in other evictions."

Seamus says that he still lives with the guilt of the impact the ordeal must have had on his children, admitting that it was a terrifying time for all of them.

"To be honest with you, it must have had a terrible effect on them, and I felt so bad that I put this on my children. I blamed myself one hundred per cent. I caused this because I wasn't able to pay what I agreed to pay. I felt so ashamed that my children were being put in danger - not only of losing their home but also of being physically hurt because of me. That's something I still struggle with."

There were times when Seamus did doubt himself, wondering if he was doing the right thing. And despite a few 'wobbles' in the first few days, he knew – with the backing of his children – that he had to take a stand.

"I did second guess myself at times, mainly because of the fear for my kids' safety. Then, of course, there was the fact that my extended family wouldn't want this all over the media when they had paid their way through life," Seamus says.

"My parents were dead, but I felt guilty that I was bringing the Sherlock name into this situation. My mom was only dead a year at the time, and I was very close to her, and I used to say: '*Thank God she's not here to see this because she'd have lost the plot.*' But in saying that, I knew she was with me every day, and she would have been proud. Then, of course, I had to consider the kids' mother, who had nothing to do with all of this, and that can't have been easy for her either.

"But the bottom line is that I always go with my gut – no matter what the situation is - and my gut feeling on this was that I genuinely believed they were wronging me. I knew I would have to work hard to pay for this, but I had nearly a third of it paid as it was, so in my mind, this was doable. I kept saying that this was possible and that I would give my whole life paying for it if I had to. I thought it was time for someone to stand up and say no. It's such a small word but such a powerful one. I always thought that if I could convince the bank to listen, they'd say, '*Okay, we'll sit down with this hoor,*' - and that's all I wanted."

It was only a matter of days before Seamus Sherlock and his family found themselves front and centre of a media frenzy - with newspaper, radio and TV journalists arriving in their scores looking for his side of the story. It was manic, and Seamus admits that he felt like a deer in headlights most of the time.

"It was absolutely crazy. So many reporters came to the gate and asked me what was happening, and all I was afraid of was that I was going to make a fool of myself or say something wrong. So I always told myself to just tell the truth and explain my situation, and that's what I did. I can still hear the click of the cameras. We were so scared because we had no experience of dealing with the media. It didn't matter who it was. Every day there were cameras on my face.

"On one occasion, RTE Primetime arrived with three trucks, and the dish went up, and this fella came over and marked an X on the ground and told me: '*That's where you're going to talk to Miriam O' Callaghan,*'" he recalls.

"Talk about shitting a brick. I was always petrified that I'd say something stupid. I was in the dark with a spotlight on my face, and I couldn't even see the cameraman. The RTE crew were very nice and told me to be calm, but I remember telling them that I wouldn't be able for it. But we got through it. The media was relentless, but looking back now, I suppose I am grateful for it because it generated huge support for what I was doing."

The support Seamus and his family received in the first few days after his story broke was overwhelming, and something Seamus says he will never be able to repay. It gave him the confidence to keep doing what he was doing.

"People started to appear from everywhere. It was amazing. The number of people who contacted us was incredible. People came with boot-loads of food and sweets for the kids, telling us to try our best and to hold tough. They didn't want anything in return, and you can't buy that kind of support.

"We had people staying at night then as well. People brought tents with them so I could get some sleep at night. It was very overwhelming. I did appreciate it because so many people backed us. Then there were the little messages and texts saying: '*We're behind you. Don't give up.*' I didn't feel so alone anymore.

"Lots of them were friends I'd met through farming. Terrible decent fellas altogether. One friend came five days a week. He gave up his life to stand with us. It's honestly bringing a tear to my eye just thinking about it. People came from all over Ireland. A neighbour gave us a timber hut, so fellas had something to sit in. There was someone with me every night. I still stayed in the jeep because I didn't want anyone to get hurt. I didn't want anyone to fight my battle for me. They kept telling me that they wanted to be part of this, and it was wonderful to hear their stories and where they came from. They didn't want anything except to stand with me. I wasn't in the right frame of mind to really appreciate that at the time, but I really do now. I was fiercely proud of those people, and I felt I couldn't let them down."

Seamus admits, however, that not all the reaction was positive and says his stance did divide people.

"A lot of people backed me, but a lot of people didn't. I got a lot of nasty phone calls too, but I respected both. I tried to explain what I was doing, and some people didn't want to know. It did hurt, of course, but these things you get over.

"I remember one fella slowed down at the gate, and he just shouted out: '*Pay your fuckin' bills, will ya*' and drove off again. I suppose I didn't blame him, really. He could have been struggling to pay his; I don't know. I think, for a while, a lot of people thought I was trying to get the farm for nothing. I think a lot of the anger stemmed from that. I was very anxious in any media interviews I did; I made it clear that I wasn't able to pay what I agreed, and all I needed was more time. Some people rang and said they couldn't wait to see me turfed out on the road. I often lay in the jeep wondering why people said what they said, but I feel they must have been hurting, or there must have been some underlying issue."

But those who did show up to support Seamus and his family massively outweighed those who didn't, and when the magnitude of what was happening was explained to them, they didn't falter. Some days there were 20 people there, some days there were two. The only day Seamus was on his own was Christmas Day.

So what *was* the plan if the bailiffs arrived?

"The plan was that the men at the gate would try to protect me, but I said from day one that there would be absolutely no physical violence. I actually asked someone to hand my gun to a dealer in Listowel for me because I didn't want to have it on me. If I had it, there was always a chance that someone could lose their head. It was the best thing I ever did because you just don't know.

"They kept telling me that if the bailiffs got me out, they'd bring me back in. But to be honest, we really didn't know what we were going to do. The honest truth? The plan was we had no real plan."

Looking back on those first initial days at the barricade, terrified that he and his children could be physically dragged from their home at any time of the day or night, Seamus gets hugely emotional:

"It was cruel. I was on full alert 24/7. I never rested. But I had to do it because I couldn't have a situation where I wasn't there when they came. I tried once or twice to sleep in the house, but I couldn't. I was too far away from the gate, and I didn't want them to burst in the door and go upstairs to me or the kids. When the girls would go out the gate to the school, they'd turn to me and say: *'Dad, you will be here now when we get back, won't you?'* It was torture.

"I was my own worst critic and would have been very hard on myself. I have never forgiven myself for putting the kids in that kind of danger. What kind of a father was I for doing this to my children? Deep down, I thought I'd never see the end of it. I couldn't see any way out of it other than them killing me. I was under 24-hour eviction notice from the day that letter arrived."

****

How It All Came Undone...

"When I lost my bog, I lost 80% of my income – but I thought I could get back on my feet."

Back in 2002, Seamus Sherlock realised a life-long dream when he bought his own farm in Feoghanagh, in rural West Limerick. The idea of buying Appletown Farm was something that Seamus had toyed with for quite a while, so he was immensely proud when he finally signed on the dotted line.

For the previous 15 years or so, Seamus had earned a respectable living cutting turf on Redwood Bog in his native North Tipperary and so felt he was in a comfortable position, financially, to expand his portfolio and buy his own farm.

"At the time, I owned a little bit of land at home in Tipperary – now I mean, very little - and I saw this farm for sale in Limerick. I had people belonging to me down there, and I always wanted to buy a bit of ground, and when I saw it, I fell totally in love with it," Seamus explains.

"I went to my accountant, and we did the figures, and I remember him telling me that I was still young but that I'd have to work hard for the next 20 years to pay it back. I was okay with that because I was cutting a considerable amount of turf and had a steady and reliable income. We were working flat out from April until July or August every year, and I had the machines put out for the winter on other jobs, so everything was going well. My accountant said to me, *'Knowing you, you're going to buy it whatever I say.'* And I did. I bought it."

Seamus saw the new farm as a new chapter in his life and one that he was very excited about. He knew that the distance from his new farm to his bog in North Tipperary would be a bit of a challenge in terms of his daily commute, but he was confident he could adapt to make it work.

"At the time, I was living in the parish of Rathcabbin in Tipperary, and when I bought the farm in Limerick, I moved down there, but I would still come up every weekday to work on the bog. It was an hour and a half's drive, but sure, that didn't mean anything to me really," Seamus recalls. "I had a lot of people buying turf from me in County Limerick, so I'd bring down a load with me every evening. "

The farm in Limerick was much more than a business transaction or financial investment for Seamus, however. It meant a whole lot more than that...

"The farm was a fresh start in life for me and my children. My late father had a good farm, and he and my mother reared 10 of us on that farm, and we all helped - the same as thousands of families in Ireland. My children were young and loved the ground and loved the animals on the farm, so it was a win-win situation. I will always remember the day I got the keys to Appletown Farm. I was immensely proud that I was able to do it and had every intention of paying for it. It genuinely never crossed my mind that I wouldn't be able to pay for it."

For the next few years, Seamus worked extremely hard on both his bog and his farm, experiencing the same challenges, trials and headaches that most self-employed landowners were accustomed to. But he was making ends meet, and life, as far as Seamus was concerned, was pretty good.

By mid-2006, however, the wheels of Seamus' business world slowly started to come off when news broke of an EU Habitats Directive which aimed to make it illegal to cut turf on 53 Irish bogs, including Redwood. Even then, Seamus never truly believed that he would lose his bog, which by then accounted for up to 80 per cent of his income.

"By 2006, everything was still going to plan, but there was talk of the bogs shutting. If I'm honest, I never took it too seriously and just thought the chance of it closing was slim. I suppose I was a bit in denial if nothing else," Seamus admits.

"By 2007, it really started getting tough, and they were saying they were going to close. I remember people started coming to the bog to take videos, and I asked them what they were doing – and they told me that my bog was soon to be a preserved bog. I just got a bit of a bad feeling.

"These lads were there every week. I'd see them coming, and I'd say: '*Oh shit, they're here again; they must mean business.*' Eventually, they were telling me that this was going to be my last year, and I used to say: '*No way - I own this bog and have worked it for years.*' Both sides dug their heels in, but the end of that story is that an EU directive is an EU directive, and they had the power to stop me."

And Seamus was right. His bog was shut down in 2008, and all he was offered in compensation was €1,500 per year. The majority of his income was wiped out, and he was devastated.

"I just couldn't believe it was happening. How could they just shut me down and take away my income? I mean, how could you go from turning a lot of money to living on €1,500 per year? It was an insult. The problem I had too was that all the machines I had were being leased, so even if I sold them, I would probably only get back what I owed on them. It was an absolute disaster. It was heartbreaking stuff."

With little or no money coming in, Seamus' health really started to suffer, particularly his nerves. He suffered from extreme anxiety – not helped by the fact that he was quickly getting into arrears on his farm loan and his machinery repayments. Threats of his credit rating being destroyed if he failed to meet these payments didn't help his mental anguish.

"I ended up selling most of the machinery and paying off what was owed on them because if I didn't pay for them, they'd come and repossess them anyway," Seamus explains. "So I went to my accountant and said that I'd have to go the bank and to try and restructure things and see what's going to happen. I kept thinking that if I could hang on, things would improve. If I'm truthful, some of it was my own fault because I kind of buried my head in the sand a bit at the beginning because I thought I'd get back cutting turf. I was fully convinced it would take me a bit of time to get back on my feet, but I would do it. But once I got into arrears, I was unable to make the repayments."

After an initial meeting with the bank, Seamus was allowed a 12-month grace period where he didn't have to make any repayments. This was aimed at helping him get back to turf cutting, possibly on another bog. He was relieved at that, but, as he says himself, those 12 months weren't long passing.

"As time went on, the bank said that this wasn't going to work anymore and that I may have to sell the farm. I just said no. I wouldn't say I was arrogant, but I was bullish that I wouldn't sell it after buying it. I was paying all along and had a good bit paid off, and I stayed trying to pay, even if it meant literally selling the shirt off my back. I wanted to keep the land. Now, a lot of people might think that was stupid or whatever, but that's the way I was.

"The farm wasn't great. I only had 52 acres, and it was a dry stock farm, and anyone will tell you in dry stock farming that if you break even, you'd be doing well. I had a good few stocks, and I sold them. When the bank stopped talking to me, I went to my solicitor and said: *'Look, I want to pay for this,'* and started making payments into an account whenever I had anything to give. Every time I sold something or had some money to spare, I paid it into the account so that the bank would see I was genuinely trying to make an effort, and maybe they might restructure the loan.

"I will say, if it was now, I'd handle things a lot differently. I was in a bit of denial, I suppose, and I thought I could work myself out of it. Between the farm and the machinery, I owed less than €500,000. At the end of the day, selling everything would have probably covered the debt that was there, but I'd have been literally out on the street with nothing. I genuinely, honestly thought I could pay for it and thought the bank would see that this guy is lodging money, and he's trying – he's not ignoring us and not turning his back on us.

"But I see now that it went on and on, and I blame myself for that because I allowed it to go on too long. I was always trying to get back into turf cutting or get back into something, so I could go back to them and say, '*Look, guys, I'm back on my feet here – we can do this.*'"

Eventually, in 2010, the matter came before the court, and Seamus consented to an order for payment against him. This, he felt at the time, meant that they would get their money back one way or another – but he still needed time. He insists that he never asked for a write-down or to not pay the loan, but he just tried to explain that he needed another few years to get the arrears up to date and begin making his repayments again.

"I went to court, and I consented to the judgement against me on the grounds that I'd get time. I wanted to work out a payment schedule that I could honour. But I suppose I ran out of time. That's what they were saying in the end. It's easy to look back now and say: '*Seamus, you made a right mess of that,*' but at the time, you're in the middle of something that you don't know much about, and you're doing your damnedest to be positive and to keep everything going. I suppose I was clutching at straws.

"I said if I get back into the bog, I'll bring all the arrears up to date as quickly as I can, and we can go back to the original plan. I suppose it was just a Plan B that I was looking for. I won't say I didn't take it seriously. I took it very seriously. But you're trying to work every day and trying to keep machines going and trying to gather money. Maybe they thought I ignored them, but I wouldn't like to think they thought that. Maybe, looking back, I should have been in contact more with them, but the type of person I was, I didn't want to be telling them a sad story with no money in my hand. For a year or 18 months before the eviction order arrived, I was still trying to talk to them and say: '*Look, I have X amount of money – can't you just take that.*' Sometimes I was robbing Peter to pay Paul, but I believed that what I was putting together meant I was honourable. But they didn't want to take a few thousand here and there, and I suppose they were well within their rights to do that too."

With negotiations at a standstill, Seamus continued to pay money into the account if and when he could but insisted that there was never any mention of possible eviction.

"There had been talks of selling the farm if things didn't work, as a last resort, but I said I believed I could pay for it if I could just have more time. All along, there was never any talk of putting me out or anything like that. There was never any talk of evicting me. Maybe I could have handled it better. Maybe I should have stayed in more contact with them - I don't know. But the letter arrived, and my whole world fell apart."

****

The debt & Despair Was Everywhere

"I never knew, with anyone I was talking to, how close they were to ending it all."

Seamus with just some of the hundreds of supporters who came to stand with him at Appletown Farm during his 350-day ordeal in 2012. Photo John Reidy

Seamus Sherlock describes himself as an ordinary countryman who never wanted anything for nothing. His debt and the dire situation in which he found himself were entirely of his own making. He has never denied that.

What he didn't realise, however, was the terrifying extent of despair that so many other people were dealing with – something which became very apparent as his story gained massive media attention across the country.

As he and his family quickly became the face of rural Ireland's fight against the banks, Seamus was inundated with calls, texts and letters from people in very similar situations – some in frighteningly desperate mental states and seeing no way out.

At one point, Seamus was getting up to 50 calls a week, mostly from men who were at their wits' end trying to deal with debt. Many of them were telling him that they felt utterly ashamed and wanted to end it all. It could happen at any hour of the day or night. It was terrifying, Seamus says, and took a huge toll on his own mental health as he was now not only trying to deal with his own situation but was also taking on the burdens of so many others.

"It was overwhelming. I was getting up to 50 phone calls a week, and lads were phoning or calling to the gate in an awful state. The longer it went on, you'd nearly spot them coming. They'd say they were there to support me, but they'd be kind of uneasy and want to have a chat with me on my own and you'd realise very quickly that they were probably in trouble themselves," Seamus recalls.

"The thing that used to stagger me was that people would ring really late at night - people I didn't know from Adam - and I'd always put myself in their shoes. They must be bad. I mean, for someone to ring a stranger and talk about their debt or whatever goes with it, they'd have to be in a fairly bad place. And fair play to them for reaching out. I never minded.

"A lot of people often asked me why I took those calls with everything I was going through myself, but if someone makes an effort to contact you, the least you can do is listen to them. I'm not saying I ever believed I could help them, but the reality was that if I rang some other man late at night who I didn't know, I wouldn't be ringing for a casual chat. You're ringing because there's something bad on your mind. Because you're desperate."

Seamus believes that those who called just wanted someone to listen and understand. Maybe they got some comfort from having someone who was in the same situation and knew what they were going through? What struck him from the majority of calls, however, was the shame and embarrassment that people were feeling.

"I knew exactly where they were coming from because we were all in financial debt for various reasons. Some people probably borrowed too much, some people were maybe a bit irresponsible, and some people just had bad luck. But the thing I heard, over and over again, was how ashamed they were of being in debt. The shame of it was the big one. They were ashamed to let anyone know they were in debt, ashamed to let friends and family know, and tended to blame themselves," he recalls.

The word 'failure' was another word that also came up in so many of these conversations, Seamus says – a feeling that rang true for Seamus himself.

"It's amazing how many times I heard the word failure and, sure, many's the time I used it myself because that is how I felt. A lot of lads would say: '*I'm nothing but a failure,*' and I would try and tell them that they weren't - that the system had failed them. When I heard people saying they were a failure or they couldn't see a solution, it always worried me. They blamed themselves for everything – for the debt, for upsetting their family. In their eyes, they could see no way out."

Seamus says that so many of the calls he got were utterly heartbreaking and showed the frightening extent of the problem right across the country. Hundreds of people were in utter despair and were terrified of losing their land, their families, and in some cases, their lives.

"I remember one morning I got a phone call from a lady in Kerry who I didn't know. She said that her husband had been on the tractor for the previous three hours, holding onto the steering wheel, crying. She was in such a state and said he wouldn't get off the tractor and asked me what she could do. They owed money to the bank and I think he just broke down. He hit a wall. She told me there were tears coming down his face. These were typical of the kinds of calls I was getting.

"Another guy rang me, an oldish man, and explained that he handed over the farm to his son four years before that and that this son went away and borrowed a lot of money and couldn't pay it back and decided one day he was heading abroad and told his father he could have the farm back," Seamus recalls. "The poor man was then left trying to deal with banks and finance companies and he hadn't a clue - he was totally, totally lost. Then he said: '*D'you know what? I wish I could just walk down to the cliffs and jump off.*'

"He said he was too old for this. He explained that he handed over the farm debt-free, but now there was more owed on it than it was worth. This was the farm that he had worked hard for all his life, and it was just heartbreaking. I told him to go and engage with the bank and explain that this had been landed on his lap. He said he didn't care about the machinery being repossessed, but he was petrified they were going to take the land. I could sense the sadness and even the tears when he spoke to me. He was totally lost and he told me his heart was beating out of his chest; he was so nervous and upset. This man was in his 70s, I'd say. My first reaction was that his son was so bloody wrong to do that, but he said the son couldn't cope with it and he got a job abroad and was gone."

The stories became so familiar – with fear, shame, and despair the overriding theme in all of them.

"I remember I was asleep in the jeep one night, and the phone rang a couple of times. I was so tired I didn't answer it at first - this was two or three in the morning. It rang again, and I answered it, and it was a chap crying on the phone. He told me he hadn't slept in a month. The bank had phoned him to say they were closing all his accounts. He just kept saying, '*I'm finished, I'm finished.*' It seemed like this guy had put his head in the sand, and when the whole thing crashed around him, he completely fell apart. He was crying on the phone, and then he said something that really scared me: he said he didn't even deserve a bullet - that the bullet would be too valuable to put in his head. I told him to relax and that it was a panic attack and asked if he had anyone he could talk to. He said he had brothers but that they'd laugh at him and think he was a disgrace. Again, this was the overwhelming feeling – shame. Shame that someone will hear you're in

25

debt. Shame that someone will think little of you because you owe X amount of money.

"I remember one evening another chap rang me and said he was in a bad way. He couldn't pay for the machines and couldn't pay for the land. And he said he couldn't even go for a pint because everyone was looking at him and talking about him. He said he wouldn't go near the mart because word had got out that he was in bother and they were all talking about him. He was paranoid, and it was easy to get that way. There are plenty of fellas who left school at an early age and went home and started working on the farm and maybe never went to college and had a kind of a quiet life. There's a world of lads out there like that who just couldn't cope.

"These were the kind of calls I got and, unfortunately, most lads I could do nothing for. But they just asked how I was coping. How was I sleeping? The questions were nearly always the same, but I always said, unless you face it head-on, you've no hope of ever coping with it. A lot of lads would ring and say they're behind on repayments on the tractor or the jeep, and I'd tell them to talk to the finance company – don't ignore them. I'd tell them to stay engaged with them. That's the mistake I made. I let things get out of hand," Seamus admits.

"I had fellas from every county in Ireland contact me. There's no doubt about it. Most farmers worried that they couldn't meet their repayments. They might have bought an extra piece of land or put up a new shed or new slatted units, and they just couldn't make the payments.

"Then other fellas would ring and never really get round to talking about what you knew they wanted to talk about. They'd talk about the weather or the price of cattle, and you'd be sitting there thinking, *'Come one, come on, let's get down to why you rang'* - and sometimes they never would. Again, going back to that feeling of shame and embarrassment."

But other times, they did talk – and some of them were at absolute breaking point. In fact, Seamus knows of at least 11 men who took their own lives in the year that he was behind the barricade.

"Some of the lads who rang me could see absolutely no way out. They couldn't see the wood for the trees. They might not have been getting on at home either. Their relationship might have been breaking down because of the pressure of money. It was scary because I never knew, with anyone I was talking to, how close they were to ending it all. Looking back and thinking of those calls, some of them were people, I believe, who were on the verge of taking their lives. During the year I was behind the barricade, I lost 11 fellas I was trying to help to suicide.

"Sad doesn't cover tragedy like that. Sad isn't the right word. Your heart would sink into your chest. You just feel that that's another life gone that could have been saved. But I never agreed when people said that a person was awful selfish to do that. I thought it was anything but selfish. Okay, you've left kids and family behind, but it's very easy to get caught up in all that emotion and start convincing yourself that people would be better off without you. I used to hear people talking like that on the phone all the time. I think a lot of those guys just couldn't see a way out. There was no other way in their eyes. That didn't happen overnight. That was a long process. And that's why, when my phone rang at any time of day or night, I'd answer it. These were genuine fellas who cared so much about what people thought of them, and they often just couldn't handle it anymore."

The pressure of these calls was huge and took a huge toll on Seamus, mostly because he was left thinking about all of these people late into the night. He was also terrified that he might say the wrong thing or give the wrong advice. The responsibility was overwhelming.

"I felt very worried that I'd say the wrong thing. It was a massive responsibility that I wasn't trained to handle. Who am I to talk to anyone anyway? I often thought about the people who rang me, and I did feel responsible. I was worried that if I said the wrong thing these lads could go to the river. That was a genuine concern. I'm not a trained counsellor or anything like that but I always said that I'd be truthful with people and say I messed up myself – that I put my head in the sand. A lot of lads just wanted to hear that and talk to someone who understood.

"In a way, taking on someone else's burden took my mind off my own problems, but in another way, the problem I had was that at night I lay awake in the jeep going through all their problems, wondering how they were. I would lay there wondering if they had tried to sort things out or why they hadn't phoned me since. In a way, it was nice to get away from my own stuff, but my head was on fire. I remember I'd wake up every night thinking of such a fella who rang or some farmer I knew who was in bother and wondering, '*Jesus how can we help him?*' But sure, I was barricaded in myself. In a way it was good to get my mind off my own worries, but then it turned out that I wasn't able to park their problems.

"I was burning the candle at both ends. Instead of worrying about myself and trying to get some rest, I was worried about other guys. The next thing you know, it's two in the morning. That certainly took its toll. My head and my body aged 20 years in that year and I'll never get that back. I felt that I burnt an awful lot of energy in that year in my head, not only going through my own worries but taking on other people's problems too. You're running on adrenalin all the time."

When Seamus did eventually settle his own case, he was asked by a local garda if he would speak at public meetings on suicide. He was genuinely taken aback by the number of people who would show up. While not all would talk to him publicly, he admits that he received numerous calls after the meetings from people seeking help. It showed him, once again, just how many people still needed help.

"The amount of people out there who still need help is so scary. I'm an ordinary fella and if people are ringing *me* they have to be in a fairly bad spot. They just need a friendly ear.

"My biggest fear is that there's an awful lot of fellas still out there, middle-aged men in particular, who are totally lost and are going into a bigger, darker hole day by day. The problem is how we get them out of it? They have to reach out for help, but a lot of these guys aren't able. They won't do it. They're not of that mindset or of that era where you reach out for help. A lot of these people have no one else.

"But it's like climbing Mount Everest. You don't look up and you don't look down. You take one step at a time and eventually, you'll get to the summit. But people tend to look up and think, *'I'll never climb that; that's too high,'* and it's the same when dealing with debt. But if they just take on one creditor at a time and try to deal with that, it's amazing how you'd get there one at a time."

Seamus says that he felt extremely proud that people would reach out to him and was always proud to help. While he may not always have been able to solve their problems, there were some success stories.

Seamus helped six families settle their cases with the bank after his own case had been dealt with and still insists that negotiation is key.

"I was proud to help. I'd always take a call and give advice and support because an awful lot of people supported me, and I kind of half thought I owed it to society. You can't buy that kind of loyalty in people, so if I could help people, I did, and I never charged a penny.

"I will always remember one couple in Galway who were losing their house. They seemed a very nice couple, and I was talking to them on the phone, and I remember the bank agreed that I could go into the negotiations with them. We met this bank man, and he said things weren't that bad, and we managed to reschedule things there and then. When we came out, the couple was in floods of tears and absolutely crying their eyes out with joy. They had been worried sick that everything was going to fall apart. Afterwards, the man got down on his knees and was balling his eyes out. I went home so happy that day. No money would pay me for the joy in their eyes.

"The stories I heard were real, human stories that show that if your mental strength gives, you're in bother. The head is very fickle. If fellas don't get help quick enough and the mental health goes, they make horrendous, life-changing decisions. The burden is savage and be in no doubt, it's happening everywhere, every single day."

Seamus with sons JJ & Dermot at Appletown Farm in 2012 – His sons were always there to support him. Photo by John Reidy

My Year of Hell on Earth

"There were days I said goodbye to my children without them even realising it."

'Da, this is for you': Seamus' youngest son JJ returns to Appletown Farm in 2012 after winning the local hurling final. Seamus always regrets not being able to go and watch his son play

When Seamus Sherlock looks back on the 350 days he spent behind the barricade at Appletown Farm; he admits that if it were to happen now, he's not sure if he could do it!

That year spent in constant fear of eviction took a huge toll on his mental and physical wellbeing, with him leaving the farm only a handful of times – most of those times to see his doctor. He says that the real impact of what he and his family endured really only hit him when it was all over, describing those 350 days and nights as hell on earth.

The pressure was so intense that Seamus endured horrendously dark days, admitting here for the first time ever that he even considered taking his own life. He was saved by what he describes as a 'divine intervention' from a nurse who phoned at that exact moment and told him how much people were depending on him.

Seamus spent every single day in absolute fear that the bailiffs could come at any time of any day and believed that the only way they would have got him out was by killing him. So convinced was he of that, that he often said goodbye to his children without them even knowing it. He had even written a note outlining where he wanted to be buried if it all went wrong.

As news of Seamus' story hit the media, he was inundated with well-wishers and supporters, all visiting him to shake his hand and wish him luck. By the first week, he had supporters staying overnight at the barricade, taking turns to be on the lookout. It was a phenomenal response to one man's plight and something Seamus vividly remembers.

"I used to stay in the jeep at night because I was afraid the house was too far away from the barricade if anyone did arrive to get us out," Seamus recalls. "I wouldn't really sleep in the jeep, as you can imagine, so I'd always be awake at daybreak. I'd get up every morning, and there were always a couple of people standing at the gate. These fellas were staying there at night in their cars, and they'd be talking and chatting. We'd boil the kettle on the fire, and I'd have a cup of tea with them. I remember we had a circular barrel with the fire in it, and that's where we'd make the tea. I don't think there was a day when someone new didn't turn up. There was always someone new coming to talk and shake hands.

"There was always a great camaraderie there. They really helped me pass the day, and I'm not lying when I say we had some serious counselling sessions at my gate with these lads. They'd talk about all sorts, from their own problems, their wives, their families – you name it, we discussed it. People came every week, and on the big days - when we were marking 50 or 100 or 150 days behind the barricade - there could be up to 50 people there at one time. It was mental. Some nights they'd be playing guitars and singing, but I wouldn't be really into that.

"I always worried about whether people's support would slacken off. And if that happened, would the bailiffs wait for a time when people weren't there, and the media had moved on to another Seamus, and I'd be easy pickings? But it never happened. People never stopped supporting me, and the media never stopped reporting on our fight. The only day I was alone out of the 350 days was Christmas Day. I mean, Jesus Christ, you can't imagine that kind of support! These men would stay in the hut at the gate or in their cars overnight and head home at 6 am after not sleeping all night. I used to feel so bad for them because they gave up their lives, you could say - some I didn't even know. They are heroes in my eyes. Heroes because not one of them wanted a word of praise. Not one of them wanted their name in the media. That wasn't why they did it. It was incredible and genuinely overwhelming."

But while Seamus was fighting the biggest fight of his life, he was conscious of trying to make things as normal as possible for his five children. The younger ones had to go to school, even though it was the last thing they wanted to do. He had to try and continue life as normally as possible for them.

"Every morning, I'd go into the house to the children and make breakfast for them, and whatever animals I had, I'd feed them. When it all kicked off in August, the children weren't at school, but from September on, I had to get them ready for school and try to organise someone to bring them because I couldn't leave. Of course, they didn't want to go, but they had to. It was so hard on them," he recalls.

"I always tried to make dinner at home for the children too, just to try and keep things some way normal. I became a dab hand at making stew - Jaysus, the stew would often last three days. I had stew for breakfast, dinner, and supper sometimes. It's good to laugh a bit at it now, but I had stew A LOT."

The children were always Seamus' top priority, and he still finds it hard to forgive himself for putting them through it all. It's something he says he may never be able to overcome.

"I kept telling them that I wanted to pay for the farm. I remember sitting at the table, and they asked me what I was going to do. I told them they better leave and stay with their mom and that I'd stay and fight this. They just said: *'No way, we're not leaving you.'* One of them asked me how bad it could get, and I told them the bailiffs could come in in the middle of the night and drag them out of their beds. I believed I was being very truthful, and maybe I was being over dramatic, but that's what you do. I remember telling the girls that they couldn't stay here, but they insisted and said: *'We're standing with you, da.'* When they said that, I knew it was the right thing to do," an emotional Seamus recalls.

"They never once mentioned being scared. I suppose they were trying to be brave for me. They were fierce brave. A lot of people called and would always say: *'Don't worry, your dad is strong, ye'll win this,'* and I suppose that helped them, but there were days they saw me very down. But not once did they ever say it was too much. I'm actually in awe of them. They are 50 times better than me because they never once told me to give up. I think they knew that their da giving up meant it wasn't going to end well.

"I used to feel so bloody guilty putting them through it. I mean, what right-thinking man would put his kids through that? They were always anxious if they left for school or to go to their mom's - worrying that their aul lad would have some kind of a hissy fit when they were gone. Or that World War Four would start when they weren't there. Some nights the girls stayed with their mom, but the boys always came home, and they'd be at me to come into the house and lay down in the bed. I tried it a few times, but I couldn't sleep. I was too far away from it all."

"I genuinely feared that I would die protecting my farm - not at my own hands, but because it was the only way they were going to get me out. So I said goodbye to my children several times without them even knowing it. I would pat them on the shoulder and say: *'Mind yourself, and no matter what happens, remember who you are and what we stood up for.'* I did it because I genuinely thought I would be killed.

"I remember many mornings I'd be talking to the children when they were eating their breakfast, and I'd be saying goodbye to them and saying, *'No matter what happens, ye are great kids and never forget that. And never forget why we are doing this.'* I told them that I thought the world of them and to never forget how important it is to stand up for what you believe is right. They probably thought I was just babbling on again, but there were several times when I really thought I wouldn't see them again. I don't know how many times I said goodbye to them."

Manning a barricade 24/7 meant that Seamus missed out on a lot of his children's lives over the course of that year. One event which stands out more than others was when his young son JJ won his first underage hurling final.

"My lads used to play hurling with Feothanagh/Castlemahon at the time, and JJ was only 14, and they won the final. I always went to their hurling games, but I didn't go to any that year. I remember when he landed back with the cup after winning, I cried my eyes out. I was so proud of him, but all I could think of was how much I had let him down by not being there to see it," Seamus recalls.

"I'll never forget when he arrived home with the cup and said: *'Da, this is for you.'* God, it meant an awful lot. It was cruelly hard. We took a picture at the gate with the cup, but I'll never forget how I felt. So proud yet so angry at myself that I wasn't there for him. I missed going to matches, going to the mart, meeting people. To be honest with you, my whole life was put on hold for a year. Some days you'd question what it was all for and if I'd have to give in in the end anyway. It was crazy, but I knew deep down in my soul that it was the right thing to do."

Another harrowing reminder of the sacrifice Seamus made by choosing to barricade himself into his farm and fight for his land came on Christmas Day 2012 when he spent the day alone – apart from a short visit from his children who had been staying with their mother. He was adamant that they have as normal a day as possible and so insisted they have Christmas dinner with their mother. Seamus had steak, chips, and onions on his own.

He had also directed all the men at the barricade to leave on Christmas Eve and recalls the day very vividly.

"I made everyone go home on Christmas Eve. They argued with me and didn't want to leave, but I insisted. There was no way anyone was going to be away from their family on Christmas Day because of me. The kids went to their mom, and I stayed on my own. So many people offered to drop me Christmas dinner, but I said no. I had steak, chips, and onions that I made myself," he recalls.

"I got up on Christmas morning and fed all the animals and said good morning to the dogs and walked around the farm. Then I went in and put on the dinner and sat on my own and ate it. Afterwards, I went out again and sat at the gate all day because that's where I was so used to sitting. I did get a lot of calls and messages from people wishing me a Happy Christmas, but I didn't see a sinner that Christmas Day, apart from my children. They came and showed me their presents and brought me a present, but I just wouldn't let anyone stay."

"I remember sitting at the hut on my own watching the cars going by, and, to be honest with you, it was the one day that I wasn't really worried about being evicted. I didn't believe they'd come on Christmas Day. I just thought, *What kind of a person would come that day?* Plus, the media would have had a field day if they came that day. So, the kids left again because I wanted them to have a bit of normality. We had no Christmas tree in the house, nothing like that. Thinking back now, I suppose it was a bit sad, but that's just the way it was."

In happier times: Seamus with his five children JJ, Bernadette, Mary Kate, Bridget & Dermot and grandson Andrew at his granddaughter Rose's christening. Seamus says he will never be able to repay his children for their unwavering supporters through his ordeal.

The Fear And Anxiety Almost Led Me To Suicide

"I was on my own with the dogs and thought it wouldn't be the worst thing in the world to end this nightmare."

Not only was Seamus Sherlock's life put on hold for the best part of a year, but he lived in a constant state of fear and anxiety that the bailiffs would come. It never, ever stopped.

"I never had a minute's peace from worrying. It was alive all the time. It could happen at any minute. The jeep wasn't the most comfortable, as you can imagine, so my mind would never stop. If the dog gave a bark during the night, I'd say: '*Oh Jesus, here we go.*' The dog would sleep under the jeep or some nights in it with me, and if she started growling, I'd say to myself: '*Here goes.*' You don't panic, really; you kind of get strong and say: '*Okay, I'm ready for this.*' But sure, I wasn't ready for it at all.

"I'd heard all sorts of awful eviction stories. I had people telling me they're going to put me out to prove a point. I knew in my heart and soul that if they came to attack me, they'd probably have to kill me to get me out. Sometimes lads were saying they'd come this week or that week and that they'd send in the heavies, so I was building myself up for it all the time. I was in a constant state of fear. I remember, if I saw lights of cars coming up the road - especially if there were a couple of cars together - I'd say: '*Oh Lord, this is it, Seamus.*' It was hell on earth.

"I suppose on a Saturday evening, I got it in my head that they'd hardly do it on a Sunday, so I'd be a little cooler and try and relax a bit more, but it didn't last long. There were always a lot of people around on a Sunday, but come Sunday evening, it all started again, and I'd think: '*God, can I really do another week of this?*' It was absolute torture because I just never knew. Sunday nights were always the toughest because people would be going home again and saying good luck and telling me they hoped I'd be okay. I'd get into the jeep at night and pull the quilt over myself and say: '*Damn it, Monday morning again tomorrow.*' I don't know what it was about Mondays, but I always reckoned they'd come on a Monday morning, and that would be it. I found Sunday nights fierce lonely."

The fear never really abated, Seamus says, but he did try to find some solace in the land itself – even if it was only for a very short time.

"My only reprieve from the whole thing was when I'd go down the field with the dogs. I have one field called Buttercup Meadow, and I don't know what it is about that field, but I always feel better there. I felt close to my parents or something, even though they were never on the farm. I don't really know. I'd sit on a stone or a log and let the world go by. I wouldn't be into meditation or anything, but I'd sit and stare at the sky, or, on a fine evening, I'd lie down in the grass and look up. In the end, I wouldn't bring my phone with me because I just needed that get away from the continuous ringing. The dogs would be running around and falling over me, and all that caper and that was my escape, whether it was only for 10 minutes or two hours.

"I suppose as time went on, maybe I did feel that the bailiffs might not come, but it never lasted long. Maybe for 10 minutes, I'd convince myself because my head needed a break, but I never relaxed because I was being told by everybody that they would come - they always come! It was strange - the longer it went on, you might think it must be a good sign that they hadn't come yet, but it was more a feeling of 'Well, no, actually, the window is closing for them, so it's going to happen sooner rather than later.'

"I often sat on the bales watching the sun coming up and thought it might be the last time I'll see this. Every evening, if I could at all, I'd watch the sunset and used to say to the dogs: 'I might not see this again.' I was always hoping the bank would agree to settle things, but for a long time, I genuinely thought the only end here was going to be a bad one. I often wonder what kind of mental effect that had on me because it went on and on for so long.

"I'd lie in the jeep at night, and I'd be thinking of my parents. I was the youngest of 10 and a late arrival. My mother always told me I was never a mistake, just a surprise. My dad was elderly when I was born, and I used to lie there remembering back to when I was 7 or 8, and I'd be out helping him on the farm. On the tough nights, I used to ask my father to look over us. To be honest, I often wondered what he'd make of all this. Would he be proud? Or would he be mortified by what I was going through? But deep down, I'd like to think he would have been proud. I never really prayed, but I'd talk to my parents and people belonging to me because I always believed they were looking out for me. I don't know; maybe it just suited me to believe that.

"My biggest worry every night going to sleep was having the strength for tomorrow. I just hoped that I wouldn't flip or do something stupid. I just took it one day at a time and never thought of a week ahead. To wake up in the morning and face tomorrow was a challenge enough. My head was burnt out from all of it. I had no doubt in my mind that if the bailiffs did come, they were going to kill me. I had even written a note at the time explaining that I wanted to be buried with my parents, and that was it."

"The one thing that was really upsetting me, though, was that, at the time, I was paying every spare penny I had into the account to try and sort all this, so I wouldn't even have had the money to pay to bury myself. That was my biggest worry. I didn't want to be a burden on anyone else. I know my family would have stepped in, but these were the thoughts that were going through my mind. I made out a will and kept it underneath the seat in the jeep; I was that sure they were going to kill me."

Amazingly, Seamus admits that there were some days when he actually wished the bailiffs would come and his nightmare would be over – whatever that meant. He had suffered untold emotional pain while protecting his farm, and, on his lowest days, he simply wanted it all to end.

"I did ask myself a few times if all this was worth dying for? It's just farmland. I loved the aul land, but deep down, I kept asking where this was going to end. I always kept telling myself I was doing the right thing – because I really believed that I was – but there were times when I wished they just bloody came in because it would have been an end to it, one way or another.

"I probably wouldn't have ended up in a good place if it had happened, but some days I just felt like I couldn't take it anymore, and I'd say, *'To Hell with it, let them come and give it their best shot.'* I'd quickly change my mind again, though, remembering that that would mean someone would get hurt and we would lose our home. But sometimes, you'd be so angry, and the waiting around was torture. I was like a fella sitting in a cell waiting to be executed but not being told what time it was going to happen. I did think, '*Just do it – get the whole thing over with.*'"

Seamus' lowest moment came about six months into his fight when he considered ending his life. He was tired of fighting. Tired of being in constant fear and living under a never-ending threat of eviction. It had taken its toll, and he admits he was in a very dark place.

"One day, I went down the fields and just said, *'Seamus, maybe you've done enough of this.'* My body was tired. My head was tired, and I started to think that if this ended now, my children would go and live with their mom, and they'd have a life, and all this craziness would stop. My body was just worn out. I was on my own with the dogs, sitting on a log, and thought it wouldn't be the worst thing in the world for me to do something here and end this Hell," an emotional Seamus admits.

"I was seriously contemplating ending my own life. It had just gotten to that stage where it was too much. My only concern at that moment was my children, but I kept saying to myself that they would accept it. It's very hard to explain, but it's like if you walk into a room and it's dark, and the door shuts behind you, sometimes it's hard to see the door to get back out of that room. You go into that dark place, and your head starts convincing you that it's time to stop this."

Thankfully, Seamus' phone rang at that very moment, and it was to be a call that would change everything. Seamus believes that it was definitely an intervention from someone - maybe even his late parents?

"I'll always remember a nurse rang right at that time and asked me how I was. I told her I was okay, but she said I didn't sound like it. I never told her what was going through my head, just that it was a tough day. She told me to remember how important what I was doing was – not just to me and my family - but to the whole country. She said that an awful lot of people were depending on me and talking about me and how brave I was."

"I don't know who sent her at that exact moment, but she probably saved my life that day. It was amazing how she rang at that exact time, really. It was her words. It had to have been an act of intervention from someone, maybe even my mother and father; who knows? That was certainly the lowest I ever got. I don't think you can get much lower, really, can you? I honestly can't say, if she hadn't phoned me, whether or not I would have gone through with it, but I was definitely considering it, and I'd be lying if I said it wasn't."

Seamus admits that it took him a while to recover from that experience and the thoughts of what might have been, but it did make him refocus on what he was doing and why.

"After that one really dark day, I started to feel that if I gave up now, I would be letting down my family and children and everyone who was rooting for me. I'd be letting down all those who stood at the gate, and I would have let myself down. So many people were supporting me, and that encouraged me to stay going. If they were willing to give up their time for me, the least I could do was keep doing what I was doing. I used to be so embarrassed, wondering why they were all doing this. *These are all depending on me.* I don't know - did we touch a nerve or what? But I knew then that I couldn't give up."

Little did Seamus know that his fight would last the best part of a year, but what he was sure of was that there was no turning back now.

"Mentally, it put a huge strain on me. I'm probably not the same Seamus I used to be. In fact, I know I'm not. I aged 20 years in that year. But I always hoped against hope that we could do this, and I can honestly say I have no regrets about what I did."

Dividing Opinion

"The support was immense, but some of the abuse was vile."

Seamus Sherlock has often conceded that he will never be able to fully thank the hundreds of people who supported him during his year-long fight against eviction: from those who sent cards, phoned him, and wrote letters with fivers attached to those who sent texts, messaged him online, not forgetting, of course, the men who joined him on the front line, often giving up their lives to show support for his cause.

What he hasn't spoken about much, however, is how his stand divided the country and how some people sent vicious messages and made vile calls that hurt him badly.

As positive a person as you're likely to meet, Seamus always takes things at face value and has always accepted that some people simply didn't like what he was doing – whatever their reason may have been.

Some things, he cannot forgive, however - like the group of young lads, still unknown to him, who called him in the early hours one Saturday morning bragging that they were sexually abusing his three daughters and asking him how brave he was now!

When he reminisces about his decision to stand up to the banks and fight for a fair right to pay for his farm, Seamus says that he knew he was never going to get full support. He was okay with that. He knew there were going to be people who would look at him as a failure and wouldn't be afraid to tell him that either. People have strong opinions.

Looking back now, Seamus admits that his stance certainly divided opinion and remembers how some people told him out straight, often with delight, how they hoped he would lose and get thrown out on his ear. It was part and parcel of what he had come to expect, he said, having put himself in the public eye by doing what he did. That didn't mean it hurt any less, but he had to put up with it.

"I've spoken before about the man who slowed down and my gate and shouted: *'Pay your fuckin' bills, you bastard'* and then just drove off. I was so shocked. If he had stopped to talk to me, I'd have explained what I was trying to do, but he didn't want to know. He was livid and didn't give a damn what I had to say. That, I suppose, was my first experience of the negativity that was out there, and there was plenty more where that came from," Seamus recalls.

"I got a lot of that, to be honest. I think a lot of people didn't know what was going on. I reckon a lot of them thought, *'This fella bought a farm, and he doesn't want to pay for it, and he expects us all to pay for it.'* There was that perception out there by lots of people - that I didn't want to pay anything. Some might only be flippant comments, but I still remember them, and they did hurt. Probably because I knew a lot of the people saying it."

"Some locals told me that they didn't want Feothanagh to be known for the wrong reasons, and I was told to fuck off back to Tipperary where I came from and stop bringing this shame on them. I suppose I had to respect their opinions because they clearly felt strongly about this, even if I didn't agree with them at all."

While the man in the jeep clearly didn't want to converse with Seamus, many others had absolutely no qualms about having it out with him. Some phoned him to tell him exactly what they thought, while others made it their business to call to the gate and let him have it.

"Oh, plenty phoned me or called to the gate purposely to abuse me – plenty. In a way, I suppose I did admire them when they told me who they were and why they were there, but some of the texts and calls were savage. I heard it all - that I was a disgrace and that I was disgracing my whole family. I was told that I had destroyed my children's future and that they would never be thought of as anything because their father was a con man and a crook, and a gangster. All this kind of stuff. That hurt terribly, and sometimes it made me doubt myself, and I wondered if this was really what people thought of me - that I'm a good-for-nothing yoke. That really hurt because, apart from it not being true, I imagined these people would be jumping for joy if I got dragged out of here. And I suppose they might have been; I don't know.

"And there were some people telling me how they hoped I wouldn't win – that they couldn't wait to see me thrown out of the house. I think a lot of people were struggling themselves and were hurting and angry. I might be wrong, but I thought maybe some of them felt I had started something that they'd have to be part of, and they didn't like that. They were very angry that I had, as one man put it, *'The fucking cheek'* to stand up. Maybe they felt that I was making them look weak because they had given in, which was not my intention at all. I mean, how do you even answer abuse like that?"

"I'd be okay during the day because I'd be up talking to someone, or I'd have animals to feed, but it's at night when I was trying to sleep in the jeep that it would all be going through my head. Maybe I was a bit too soft, and I should have been toughened to that, but I always cared a lot about what people thought of me."

Seamus recalls a conversation he had with a good friend of his about a year after he had settled his case and how what that friend revealed shocked him to his core.

"I had a very good friend who I knew ever before any of this started. He was a really good guy, and he came to the farm a few times. A really nice guy. But he told me something afterwards that shocked me. He rang me about a year after it was all over and asked if we could have a chat. He said he had something to tell me. Then he said, *'I hated your guts for doing what you did.'*

"I got some shock. He said he knew that if it had happened to him, he wouldn't have had the balls to do it and that he had hoped I'd lose. He told me that if they had come to his farm, he'd have given it to them and that if I had won, then everyone would have to stand up, and he hated me for that. He apologised afterwards and said he was so wrong for thinking that way, but I was just so taken aback when I heard it. Even when he was there with me and bringing food, he really must not have wanted to be there. Then I started to ask myself if a lot more people felt like that."

"There were times I often spent two or three hours thinking that way. I started to think whether or not the people who stood with me really believed in me and in what I was doing, or did they also think I was a bollox? Will they have a party when I'm dumped out of here? But that's just your mind – the stupid part of your mind – doing overtime. Then I'd say, *'No, these people are genuine,'* and I'd just try to put it to the back of my mind."

While Seamus was getting used to the nastiness and trying to navigate his way through a frenzy of newspapers, tv, and radio interviews - which he admits were almost always fair and honest - one call from a national newspaper absolutely knocked him for six.

"The person at the other end of the phone introduced themselves as a journalist from a national newspaper and asked me if I'd answer a few questions. I said, 'No problem,' but what they said next scared the absolute life out of me," Seamus recalls.

"They asked me if it was true that I beat my children and locked them in the attic. They insisted that I *'tell the truth'* because they were going to print the story anyway, so I might as well say something. That absolutely broke me. I was petrified and thought if they print these lies, I'm finished. Thankfully the story never materialised, but that call set me back a long way. I genuinely thought I was done."

As horrendous as that phone call was, it wouldn't compare to a terrifying call Seamus received in the early hours of one Saturday morning as he tried to get a few hours' sleep in his jeep. It was from a group of laughing young lads claiming to be sexually abusing his three daughters, the youngest of whom was only 13 at the time. To this day, Seamus doesn't know who called him - as it was from a private number - and says he doesn't like to think what he would do to them if he were ever to find out.

"I never told my children this at the time, but it was about 3 am on a Saturday morning, and my phone rang. I was half asleep, but I could see it was a private number, and I answered it. A young fella asked: *'Is that the brave Mr Sherlock?'* I was half asleep and just said 'Yeah' without thinking. Then he said: *'We have your three daughters in the car, and guess what we're doing to them?'* They were laughing and giggling in the background. I absolutely panicked. My girls always went to their moms on a Saturday night, but of course, at that hour of the morning, when you're half asleep, you automatically question if it could be possible.

"Then he said: *'How brave and proud are you now, you bastard?'* They were laughing, and I could even hear a girl's voice in the background. Of course, I was stupid to believe it, and, looking back afterwards, I shouldn't have thought for one second that it was genuine. But it hurt more than anything because my children meant everything to me, and, in my stupidity, I believed it for a couple of minutes. But at 3 o'clock in the morning, when you're tired and worn out, it was terrifying."

"I mean, I had had some very dark days myself, but that was absolutely the worst experience I had at the hands of someone else. For someone to ring me and tell me they were abusing my girls in a car – I mean, how low can a person go?

In my right mind, I knew it wouldn't happen because the youngest one was too young to be out anyway, but they just caught me on the hop. It was so orchestrated because I could hear girls in the background. If ever I was going to get a heart attack, it was that night. They won. They got their kicks. Then the fuckers just hung up, and I never knew or found out who it was.

"I asked the girls in the morning if they were out the night before, and they said no, of course, but I never told them about the call. I could take nasty calls about myself and how useless I was, but to do that with the girls - how could anyone be so sick?"

Seamus says that while some of the abuse was vile and often uncalled for in many cases, he took immense comfort from those who did show their support. While he admits that it was 70/30 in terms of positive and negative reactions, he tried to focus on the good stuff. It's what kept him going on those dark days when he questioned what he was doing and whether it was all worth it.

"I'd say sixty to 70 per cent of the country were for me, and thirty were against. And I'm not for a minute criticising anyone for that. They just didn't believe in what I was doing, and that's totally fair enough. From where I was looking, I felt I divided the country," Seamus admits.

"I suppose it was a shock to a lot of people because it's not something a lot of people would be used to. A lot of people were kind of puzzled because they knew nothing about it. But the positive stuff was overwhelming, and that's what I tried to focus on because people went out of their way to support me. Some of the neighbours came to me and said, *'Seamus, are you alright? What are you going to do?'* And I said I was going to fight. I'd ask them whether, if push came to shove, maybe they'd show a bit of support - and they said they would. I am so proud and grateful to the people of Feothanagh who supported me and whose support never weaned over the year."

And support him they did – in their hundreds. Letters, cards, phone calls, texts, Facebook messages, and visits to the gates; he had hundreds of people backing his fight - men and women of all ages from all over Ireland and beyond. It was overwhelming and something that Seamus says encouraged him to keep fighting.

"The positive was very positive, but the biggest shock to me was the number of people who came from far away. I kept asking myself why they were supporting me. Sure, I didn't know half of them. I just think that I just struck a chord with them, maybe?"

"I remember an elderly man in Kerry, in his 90s, sent me a handwritten letter saying that he was glad he wasn't dead before he witnessed someone standing up to the banks. He had stapled a five-euro note on the corner. He said it was all that he could afford but that I could have it. That had a huge impact on me, and I remember thinking, *'I can't let these people down. They're rooting for me and my children.'*

"I got the impression that a lot of lads were pissed off themselves, and they wanted to give the bank a kick, but they were going to let me do the kicking. I never asked any of them to come, but they just kept coming. Some came once or twice, and that's fair enough - and more than I ever expected - but others came once a week, once a month. Not to mention all the lads that stayed with me every night. It was something else.

"I got an awful lot of calls and handwritten letters, and a lot of that was coming from elderly people who maybe thought that kind of an Ireland was gone – when somebody would stand up for something they believed in. Every one of those letters meant an awful lot to me. In ways, it put a bit of pressure on me because I was thinking that these people were depending on me, but it meant the world that someone would go to the bother of writing a handwritten letter. I don't know how many people stapled money to the corners and told me to buy something nice for myself and the kids."

'The letters were hugely encouraging,' Seamus says, especially those willing him on and telling him to have faith and belief in what he was doing. Many others, mostly strangers, spoke of how proud they were of Seamus, which was hugely emotional, he admits.

"To be honest with you, some of them made me cry because they were handwritten, and you'd know in your heart and soul that it took a lot for that person to sit down and do that. A lot of them didn't want to know my financial details, and they were just telling me to keep strong and mind the children. A lot of them were romancing the old Ireland, but it was always so nice to open the envelope. It made me feel very proud to be Irish, to be honest with you. I was also relieved that people believed in me and didn't think I was some lu-la looking for attention. I think it made me more determined to hold on as long as I could. Reading things like

'Keep going, keep strong, don't let them beat you,' meant a lot to a fella like me who was barricaded inside a gate. I remember one letter, it didn't say who it was from, but it just said *'I wish my father and mother were alive to see this.'* It was that short, but that meant a lot to me."

About a year and a half after Seamus' ordeal was over, he made what many might consider a somewhat unusual decision to get rid of all the letters. He did it for closure, he says, but was adamant about doing it in a way that, he felt at least, respected every single person who went to the trouble of writing to him.

"About 18 months after it was all over, I dug a hole on the farm, and I burnt all the letters. The reason I did that was that they were no one's business but mine and the people who wrote to me. I said the ashes can go into the land that we fought for, and the memory is always there," Seamus explained.

"I took everything to do with that case and burnt it. I remember I sat there and watched it burn, and when all that was left was ashes, I just covered it over. What I was trying to do was just get my mind off it. I was trying to come back to some kind of normality because I was still thinking night and day about what I'd been through. I just thought, *'That battle is won now, so maybe it's time to put this to bed and try and get back to my life.'* To try and move on for want of a better word. Every day, after it was all over, I'd open a drawer looking for something, and I'd see a letter, and it would bring me straight back to the whole thing again, and I'd think, *'Jesus, I'll never be able to thank all these people.'* I have strange ways of doing things, I suppose, but I just thought that these letters will be part of this farm long after I'm gone."

Looking back now, Seamus says that the support he received from so many people was what kept him going, admitting that he's not sure if he would ever have gotten over the finish line without them.

"The support I got and the volume of letters I received - the majority from strangers - kept me going, without a doubt. If I had been there on my own and no one was coming to visit or sending me these letters, I'm not sure if I would have lasted. No matter how tough you are – I don't care if you're the Bull McCabe – you just couldn't do it."

"In the mornings, there was a woman who'd pull up with rashers and sausages and bread for all the lads at the gate. Another man dropped cooked chickens three or four times a week, every week. And I mean, he had to drive into Tesco and do that. There were so many people doing things like that. It was nearly embarrassing, but it meant the world to me. I often said that if I don't get killed by the bailiffs, I'll die of a heart attack; I was eating that many rashers and sausages," Seamus joked.

"Then there were people going to mass on a Saturday night, and they'd stop off with a bag of shopping when they were passing. There could be donuts or buns or bars of chocolate. I didn't know who did it half the time. It was so nice and meant so much at the time. I can't thank those people enough. Everyone, in their own little way, gave us a push that we needed on a particular day. What I couldn't understand was that this was my fight with the bank – *so why was everyone else helping? Why would they care?"*

"But it showed me that Ireland is still full of great people. And without them, I simply wouldn't have survived."

It's All Over…

"They told me they had agreed to my proposal, and I went down on my knees and cried."

Seamus stands at the gate of Appletown Farm recently, recalling the moment his fight was finally over, and he was allowed to open the gate after a 350-stand-off. Photo by Andrea Etter

Day 350 of Seamus Sherlock's stand against his eviction began like all the others before. He had fed the animals and was in the kitchen having his breakfast when his phone rang. Nothing new there – his phone never stopped ringing - and the fact that it was a private number wasn't unusual either, so he answered it.

But instead of a reporter or another farmer looking for help and advice, this time, the call was from a representative from the bank telling Seamus, ever so briefly, that they had accepted his recent proposal to settle his debt.

That was it! Seamus was floored. He didn't even get a chance to question what had just happened before the caller hung up, but from what he had gathered in the 20-second call, his fight was finally over. It was a call that he had not expected that morning but one that he says he will never, ever forget.

"I was in the kitchen having a cup of tea, and a private number rang me. I just answered it, like I always do, and they asked if that was Mr Sherlock. I said it was, and he said he was ringing from the bank to tell me they had agreed to my proposal. That's all he said…and then '*goodbye*,' Seamus recalls.

"I was totally caught on the hop and genuinely didn't know what to do. My heart started thumping, and I said, *'God Almighty, I think they've just agreed?'* I just couldn't believe it. The tears just burst out of my eyes. I was on my own, and I was uncontrollable. I just couldn't believe this was happening. It didn't sink in at all. *Could this possibly be over?*"

Seamus immediately rang his son Dermot to tell him what had happened, and while he waited for him to come home, he went down to the lads at the gate to tell them the unbelievable news. He laughs now as he recalls how unsure he still was about the whole thing and how he relayed the call to the men who had spent the previous night with him, protecting his farm.

"I went running out to the gate, and there were a couple of lads out there, and I said, *'I think this is over.'* They looked at me and said, *'What do you mean you 'think' it's over?'*

and I explained how I had just got a call to say they had accepted my offer…that they had agreed. They asked me again if I was sure, and I said, *'Well, yeah, I think so.'* I said, 'I'm after getting a phone call,' and they've agreed. It happened so fast, and I was so bloody tired from being barricaded in there so long; I was in a mess, to be honest."

As amazing as it was to tell the lads at the gate that his battle was finally over, it was Dermot's arrival back to the farm that saw Seamus completely break down. The torment and unbelievable anguish that he and his family had endured for almost a year came rushing back to him when he saw his son in front of him - his son who had stood by him from day one. He simply couldn't contain his emotions.

"Dermot came home, and he looked in the door and asked me if it was really over. I just couldn't even get the word yes out of my mouth. I know that sounds silly now, but I just went down on my knees and started crying. I remember he was patting me on the head, saying, *'You're grand da, you're grand.'* I swear, I couldn't control myself. The relief. I often heard people talking about financial debt being like an ESB pole on your shoulder, but it's way more than that. Your whole demeanour is crushed. I'll always remember I was kind of embarrassed that I couldn't get the words out to Dermot. I was uncontrollably sobbing. It was an amazing feeling. It's so hard to explain it properly."

After almost a year behind the barricade, Seamus recalls the extraordinary moment when he eventually opened his gate again. Despite that morning's phone call seemingly telling him the standoff was over, he admits that he was still extremely nervous and a little unsure whether or not it was a ploy by the bank to catch him out.

"I actually said to myself: *'God, am I pre-empting this? Am I doing this too quickly?'* Seamus admits. "But I did it, and I'll never forget that feeling. It was so emotional. I just couldn't believe that it was over. I remember I couldn't find the key for the padlock of the gate - it was locked so long - so I had to cut it off. I remember the feeling when I clicked the latch opened. My God, I don't know how to explain it. It was pure and utter relief. I can still hear the sound of the latch in my head. It was just unbelievable. The gate was open, but it was so much more than a gate opening - it was opening a whole load of emotions too."

"Halfway down the drive way, I stood back, got my phone and took a picture. I stood there for an hour, I'd say, looking at it. The pure relief. I could nearly feel the tension leaving me and normal feelings coming back again. Halfway down the driveway, I looked back and saw it open. It was just amazing. It wasn't that I'd won anything, but it meant everything to me.

"I remember I stood out on the main road and said, *'My God, I can actually stand here now!'* I took a picture of the gate, and it was unbelievable. It was wide open for the first time in 350 days. To everyone else, it was just a gate, but to me, it was such a powerful picture. For weeks afterwards, every chance I got, I went and stood at the gate - even for five minutes - and said, *'Yeah, it's open, Seamus. You did it.'* "

While the gate at Appletown Farm was open again for the first time in 350 days, it wasn't until later that evening that Seamus removed the barricade – a barricade that had stood for so much for so long. He admits, however, that he was still extremely nervous.

"I actually didn't move the bales until later that day. I went down, and the gate was open, and I said, *'God, would they ever come now that I've let my guard down?'* I was totally wired. I moved the bales on my own with the tractor, and I remember I was going mad because all the bales were burst. I was walking in, and they were all a mess. Then I said, *'Will you cop yourself on Seamus? - This is the least of your worries. It's over. It's actually over.'*"

Once the realisation set in that his year-long fight was finally over, Seamus took some well-earned time to reflect and enjoy the moment.

"It was numbness for the first few hours. I think it had built up for so long, and I thought of my parents and my sister, who were now dead, and I wanted to be close to them. I brought the dogs down the field for a walk, and I looked around and said, *'Beejaysus, we're staying here.'* The dogs were all jumping around – you'd swear they knew what was happening. I'll always remember I rang a good friend of mine in Millstreet - he used to come up to me a lot - and I said it's all over. He told me he was proud of me and, I swear, I couldn't keep in the emotion. I'm not someone who tears up too easily - none of us would be - but it was just the relief of it all."

And Seamus' friend wasn't the only one to express his pride. Seamus' children, who had been their dad's biggest supporters through all of this, were understandably overjoyed that their life could finally return to some semblance of normality at last.

"Ah, the children were just so delighted. Bridget came in and gave me a hug, and they were jumping around the kitchen. It was unforgettable. But I kept reminding them that we didn't get the farm for nothing. We got the right to pay for it. It wasn't as if someone rang and said, *'Seamus, we're after paying the bill for you.'* A lot of people would say that isn't much to jump around about - but for us, it was everything. It was what I had stood for from day one."

There was one person, however, who Seamus missed dearly at that very moment, which in a way brought a veil of sadness to what was a hugely happy and proud day for the Sherlock family:

"My mother had died in 2011, and I just wished she had been there to see it. I suppose I wouldn't have wished her to be there all along because she would have been petrified, but I really felt close to her that day and would have loved to have been able to celebrate with her."

But they did celebrate – albeit in typical understated, low-key Sherlock fashion.

"We're not big into celebrating, but the kids were there that evening, and I remember we had tea and cake. I drove into town and got some aul cake, and we just sat around together. I didn't tell the kids at the time, but there was still a little bit of doubt in my head. I think that's why I went and got the cake - trying to convince myself. They were all smiling, and the girls were crying, saying, *'Da, you won.'* I just remember saying, *'No - we won.'*"

"Looking back, I don't think win is even the right word. We achieved what we set out to achieve. Bridget was crying as well, and she said, *'Dad, we're so proud of you.'* My children's respect meant more to me than anything if you know what I mean. I blamed myself for putting them through everything, so to have them say that they were proud of me meant everything."

Seamus admits that it took him a few weeks to come down from the high of that day, having fought so long to save his farm. He remembers people telling him how he'd sleep well that night but admits he didn't sleep properly for the week!

As news broke of the end of Seamus' fight, his legion of supporters was quick to congratulate him, with many returning to the farm to shake his hand. 'It was wonderful,' he says, to see them take the time to come back and express their best wishes. The public's support meant so much to Seamus and was something, he says, often got him through the darkest days.

"By the next day, it was all over the front pages, and I was on Vincent Browne that night, so a lot of people started ringing and congratulating me and saying fair play. It was an absolute whirlwind. Then my friends started calling and shaking hands, and a lot of reporters called. To be honest with you, when they called, I was still on a kind of a high.

It's only now, when I look back, that I realise and appreciate more all the highs and lows that I went through in that year.

"To think that one day I came so very close to doing something that would have changed everyone's life for a long time, but then to hang on and another day to open that gate. That is very emotional to think about."

Seamus admits that readjusting to 'normal' life wasn't as easy as one might think, likening the previous 350 days to be 'institutionalised.' It took time to get back to life as he knew it before the barricade, and that was something that caught Seamus very much off guard.

"You get used to people calling, and then, when it was all over, no one called, and that was strange. It's like I had been institutionalised. I have to be honest; I missed the people calling and the lads at the gate. So many people had sided with us. I just think it was a roller coaster thing. During the stand, some nights, I'd be in the jeep, and I'd hear the lads at the gate, and I'd think, '*I'd say them hoors are having deadly craic.*' And you can be sure there were a few drinks involved too, the hoors. They'd get up in the morning and stoke up the fire and throw on the sausages. How we didn't poison ourselves, I'll never know, but my God, they tasted nice! I did miss that afterwards, yeah."

"After a couple of weeks, you'd imagine you should be happy that it's over, but you don't come out of that overnight. I didn't anyway. Six months after it was over, I was still affected by it. It took an awful lot out of me, physically and mentally.

"This might sound a bit mad, but in some ways, it all came too quick in the end, and a lot of it went over my head. Sometimes I wonder if I thanked people enough, and I know I missed half of them. People who did so much for me, who I didn't get round to ringing to personally thank. For all the people who never wanted or expected thanks but never received it either - they meant the world to me. People brought food, dog nuts, and cattle nuts and didn't do it for thanks, but I'd like to thank them most sincerely. And, of course, those who are no longer with us. They all played a huge part in our story and can't be forgotten either."

Being a 'free man' was something that Seamus did learn to enjoy, however, and as he looks back on his extraordinary ordeal, the overwhelming feeling is one of pride.

"Within two or three months of the barricade coming down, there was such a difference when I would walk the dogs. I was a free man rather than a man barricaded in, petrified that they could arrive at any moment. A lot of people would ask me if I realise what I achieved, and yes, I do realise the magnitude of what we did. But I never thought of it as this amazing thing to do because I was embarrassed that I got myself into it in the first place.

"I never counted myself as a hero or anything like that. Absolutely far from it. But I was extremely proud of what we did and of my friends and children who stood with me from day one. I'm extremely proud of the Irish people, too, for their amazing support.

"Of course, there was negative stuff, but so many people were fiercely proud of what we had done, and that's how we felt too. We had achieved what we had set out to achieve and were going to be able to keep our farm and get a chance to pay for it."

"I never ever wanted glory, but the support of so many people helped me settle in my head that I was right for doing what I did. Sometimes I still ask myself, *'Holy shit, did we really do that?'* and I'm so extremely proud to say: *'Yes. Yes, we did.'*"

End of An Era

"There will always be a piece of my heart on Appletown Farm."

End of An Era - Seamus made the difficult decision in 2022 to sell Appletown Farm, but walks away with no regrets. Photo by Andrea Etter

In March 2022, Seamus and his family made the extremely difficult and emotional decision to put Appletown Farm on the market – the farm he fought so hard to keep ten years previously.

Having moved to Offaly to live and work full-time alongside his partner Andrea running Belmont House Stud, Seamus decided that selling the farm in West Limerick made 'commercial and common sense.'

'That didn't make the decision any easier,' he says, admitting that it was the most difficult decision of his life.

"I had huge emotions about selling Appletown Farm, but, unfortunately, I believe that you just can't make a living on 50-60 acres anymore. That farm could have raised a whole family years ago, but that day is gone now. It was the most difficult decision of my life to sell, but it was the right thing to do."

"When I moved to Offaly, I found myself driving up and down to the farm, two hours each way, and I was mentally drained and tired of it. I had no energy to do anything when I got there. So, I spoke to the family, and we decided together that we'd put it up for sale and buy a farm up in County Offaly, not far from where I'm living now.

"It made commercial and common sense because I'm originally from North Tipperary, and two of my sisters and brothers are there. My other two sisters live in Dublin with their families. We bought the new farm on March 4th, and JJ will move up and help farm it. Dermot has already moved to the area in the last 12 months with work, so the two boys are close, which is great."

"It won't really have a huge effect on the girls – Bernadette is a psychiatric nurse; Bridget is working in childcare, and Mary Kate is in college - so they will come up here to me instead of Appletown at weekends."

Seamus is understandably emotional when he reflects on the decision to sell the farm that had such a huge impact on his life and says that a piece of his heart will always be on Appletown Farm.

"It was a huge decision, and I had a lot of sleepless nights weighing it all up, but I have no doubt that, regardless of who buys that farm, there will always be a bit of my heart there. I couldn't just walk away from it completely.

"No matter who owns it, they're getting my farm, but they're also getting a bit of my heart with it. My heart will always be on that farm – I know every inch of it. I walked every inch of it. I fought for it. So, there is no way I could walk away from Appletown Farm, body and soul.

"I'm still full of mixed emotions if I'm honest, but there are many happy emotions too, and I feel that it's onwards and upwards now. We have a new, bigger farm, and I'm working full-time on the stud farm at Belmont House, and I've really embraced that 100%, so that makes the decision a little easier."

Seamus and his sons JJ & Dermot on their new farm in County Offaly. Photo by Andrea Etter

Appletown Farm is currently on the market, and while Seamus admits that he will be extremely emotional when the sale is complete, he is at peace with his decision.

"I'm a firm believer that the wheel of life is always turning, and it starts when you're born and finishes when you die. For me, that's very obvious; I think: In 2002, I bought the farm; in 2012, I was barricaded in trying to protect it, and in 2022, I made another huge decision to sell the farm. So that wheel is always turning. But for me, I feel that I'm now coming back to my roots – and I'm at peace with that."

Seamus enjoying his new life on the farm in 2022. Photo by Andrea Etter

Was It All Really Worth It?

"I'd sooner die standing than live on my knees."

THIS year marks the 10th anniversary of Seamus Sherlock taking his extraordinary stand against the eviction order that he always believed was unjust.

Revealing that he is now in a very happy place with his partner Andrea, running Belmont House Stud with her, Seamus still looks back in disbelief at what he actually went through. Sadly, he says, he will never be the person he was before his tortuous year behind the barricade began but admits that if he had to do it all again, he probably would!

"I was down on the farm recently, and I parked at the gate, and I just sat there trying to imagine what I did there for a year. It was putting hairs on the back of my neck, and I was saying: *'Did I really do that? Did I actually sleep here every night? I must have been absolutely bloody crazy.'* But you do what you have to do at the time.

"But I can see now that the whole ordeal took the sparkle out of my eye, if I'm honest. It was just an unbelievable struggle. Will I ever get back to where I was before it all? *No.* But I'm glad to be alive, and I'm glad everything turned out the way it did.

"I've often asked myself a few times since, *Was the land worth it?* And sure, I suppose it was. But I have lost the bit of fun that was in me. I unwillingly gave everything up to fight for that year, and that's sad, I suppose. You don't get back that feeling. Looking back, it's only now hitting me exactly what I did."

"When I settled my case, people would come to me for financial help, and I threw myself in at the deep end straight away. I never gave myself time to digest and grieve for what I had been through - if grieve is the right word. I should have taken a year or two out to get over what I went through myself - just to chill, I suppose. I never really got over what I actually went through."

"Up until three years ago, I was still helping people all the time, but in the end, I just hit a stone wall. I was driving to Louth and Donegal to meetings and was going as far as the Beara Peninsula speaking to farmers. To be honest, I was all over the place. It was very tough because when people wanted your help, you felt you had to do it. But one morning, I just decided that I'd had enough. I don't know, I just didn't have the heart to do it anymore. It was never-ending. My head was fried. I was getting 50 calls a week, no bother, and I jumped into it headfirst. I just needed time out, and it was the best thing I ever did."

"I suppose it went some way towards me giving something back to the people who came and supported me. But I was exhausted. Saying that, if you rang me in the morning and said: *'Seamus, I have a guy down the road there in a bit of bother, can you help him?'* I'd still take the call, of course. But I won't go running and racing the roads anymore."

Despite the extraordinary ordeal Seamus went through, and the subsequent mental and physical exhaustion he suffered as a result of travelling the country to help others, he admits that life is good now.

He and his children have moved on from the drama of that unforgettable year and are very happy – and he is happily taking it at a much slower pace.

"I'm definitely in a good place now - a very good place – but the whole thing had a serious effect on my health, and I'm not going to lie and say it didn't. But I'm alive, in a very happy relationship, and the kids are all doing great living their own lives, so we take every day as it comes."

"Thankfully, they all seem to be getting on very well, but even now, I still ask them now and again if it all affected them. They all say no - just that they were worried for me. Thankfully, they're young and full of beans and seem very happy, which is all I ever want for them."

"I'm very happy too; thanks be to God. I'm working full-time on Belmont House Stud, living with a very nice lady, and we get on like a house on fire. I'm happy with our decision to sell Appletown Farm and buy a new farm here. I will always be a man of the land, and the land means everything. Picking up that bit of clay in your hand and rubbing it into a ball - that's what soothes my head."

"Things are good, yeah. The children and I have a great relationship, and they still come to me - especially for the money! Technically speaking, I'm free, and I think my head is in a very good place now."

Looking back now at the horrendous ordeal that he and his family endured, you might think that if it were to happen again, Seamus would do things differently. 'Not so,' he says because he firmly believed in what he was doing.

"The only regret I have, if that's even the right word, is that I probably should have tried to make a better effort to meet the bank more. But if I got an eviction letter again in the morning, would I stand again? I would - If I believed in it. You have to be true to yourself, and I always went with my gut and with what resonated in the bottom of my stomach."

"But would my body or my head take it again? *I don't know.* Back then, I was going into the unknown, so I didn't know what I was doing. It was one day at a time. I thought when I barricaded the gate that it was going to be over in two or three weeks, one way or another. I thought that my stance was either going to force them to throw me out or deal with me quickly. I never for the life of me thought I'd be there 350 days later."

"I lived day by day, and my biggest problem is that I don't fear anything. I'm not sure if that's a good way to be, but I have no fear of death because I lived an extraordinary life. So, if I go tomorrow, so be it - I'm going to enjoy today."

Seamus says that he is extremely proud of how the Irish people stood by him throughout his fight, describing his supporters as the unsung heroes in this extraordinary tale. He is also hugely humbled that his fight inspired others not to give up.

"I remember going to my doctor one day, and he commented that I was very down in myself. I told him I wasn't really sleeping, and what he said next will stay with me forever. He said, *'The next time the monkeys appear in my head at night, tell them I know of two men who come into this same surgery who are alive because of you. Their children have a father because of you.'* I cried going home in the car that day thinking about that. I was embarrassed at the time, but he would not have said it unless it was true."

While Seamus has never shied away from expressing how disappointed he was that the bank decided to take such drastic action and issue an eviction notice, he says he has let any resentment go for the sake of his own mental health.

"I've let it all go. I never slated the bank. That wouldn't achieve anything. I don't carry anger, and I am not a hateful person. The only person I blame for this is myself. If I had been able to pay what I agreed on day one, I wouldn't have been in this mess."

"But I'll be honest; I wasn't happy with the way I was railroaded. But I'd be an odd aul character that way. If you bully me at all, I'd be a devil for digging my heels in. But I don't carry any resentment now."

"Saying this, I still have the scars of what I did - mentally and physically. But at the end of the day, I'd sooner die standing than live on my knees."

Seamus is thoroughly enjoying his new life at Belmont House Stud

Photo by Zsofie Denes

Reminiscing on his 350-day stand against eviction, Seamus says he will never be the same person. But will always be so proud of what he did. Photo by Andrea Etter

Lightning Source UK Ltd.
Milton Keynes UK
UKHW022039080922
408568UK00006B/180